AMAZING DAYS

Notable days

for

extraordinary classrooms

JOAN
O'CALLAGHAN

Amazing Days
Notable days for extraordinary classrooms
by Joan O'Callaghan

2nd Print Edition 2016, Carrick Publishing
Print Edition 1991, Scholastic Canada Ltd.
Copyright Joan O'Callaghan, 1991, 2014, 2016

Cover Design by Sara Carrick

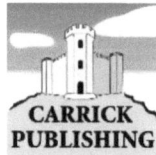

CARRICK
PUBLISHING

ISBN: 978-1-77242-051-7

CONTENTS

SEPTEMBER

SEPTEMBER 1

On this day in 1968, a school for training circus clowns was established in Florida. It was the first school of its kind and offered a free eight-week course covering subjects such as slaps, falls, juggling, stilt-walking, make-up and pantomime.

Clown Faces

Materials needed:
yellow, blue, pink, red, orange and green construction paper
tape
a stapler

Directions
Cut out the following:
two blue star shapes
one yellow circle, one red circle and four orange circles
    (5 cm in diameter)
one green triangle
one pink clown-shaped mouth

How to put it all together

Fold two large square sections of the newspaper like an accordion, using 5 cm folds. Fold each "accordion" in half to make fan shapes, then staple the flat sides of the fans together to form one big circle. Attach the yellow circle to the tip of the triangle to make the clown's hat and cut the orange circles in continuous spirals to make the clown's hair.

Attach the mouth, the hat and the hair to the clown's face. Then glue on the red circle for the clown's nose and the star shapes for the eyes.

Extended Activity

Invite the children to choose names for their clowns, and have each write or tell a little story about what it must be like to be a circus clown. The stories can then be shared orally or written out and attached to each clown.

Books

Circus Time by Connie Klayer and Joanna Kuhn, Scholastic, 1979
Jumbo, The Biggest Elephant in the Whole World, by Frances McLaughlin Burns. Scholastic, 1978.

SEPTEMBER 4

In 1876, Frederic Stupart issued the first Canadian-prepared storm warning from the headquarters of the new Meteorological Service of Canada in Toronto.

Prior to this, trains used to carry large metal discs on their baggage cars or engines to provide weather forecasts for people living within sight of the railway. The shape of the disc indicated the nature of the forecast. A full moon predicted fine weather, a star meant rain and a crescent moon called for showers.

Weather Discs

Tell the children about the trains and the discs they used to carry, then invite them to design their own weather discs for today's weather. Encourage them to share their completed discs with the rest of the class and ask them to explain their choice of symbols.

Extended Activity

Discuss the way we get our weather information from TV, radio and newspapers and let the children take turns being class meteorologist for a day. In addition, we now use the Internet as an excellent resource.

SEPTEMBER 8

Today is International Literacy Day and it's a good time to promote a love of reading in your classroom.

I Want To Read About...

Try some of the following with your class
* Set aside some time each day for USSR (uninterrupted silent sustained reading).
* Invite each child to bring his/her favorite book to class or read the group one of your favorites.
* Make a classroom big book entitled *Our Favorite Books*. Have each child contribute a drawing of one of the illustrations from his/her favorite book for each page.

Books

The Reader's Catalog, edited by Geoffrey O'Brien. Jason Epstein, 1989.

SEPTEMBER 12

In 1972 the government established Heritage Canada as a national trust to preserve historic buildings, natural areas and scenic landscapes in Canada.

The Way It Was

Explain to the students what we mean when we talk about heritage. Show them pictures (or PowerPoint) of local heritage spots or visit an historic site.

Explain that within our families we have a heritage as well, which includes things like family stories, antiques and favorite toys and recipes.

* Invite each child to bring in and talk about an item (or a photograph of an item) that's part of his/her family heritage.
* Have the children make recordings or drawings of favourite family stories.

Books

The Velveteen Rabbit by Margery Williams. Scholastic, 1990.

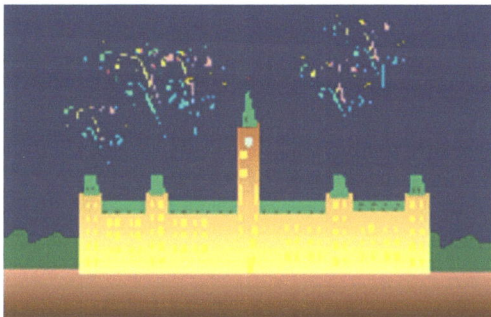

SEPTEMBER 13

In 1847 Milton Hershey, the founder of Hershey's chocolate candy, was born.

What's in a Word?

Print CHOCOLATE on the blackboard, then ask the children to discover how many smaller words it contains. How many words can they make by rearranging the letters?

SEPTEMBER 14

On this day in 1658, in the midst of a great storm, Sir Isaac Newton tried to calculate wind speed by measuring the difference between how far he could jump against the wind and how far he could jump with the wind.

On the Wind

Make wind chimes out of clothes pegs.

Books

The Wind in the Willows, by Kenneth Grahame. Scholastic, 1989.

Internet

In addition to your local library, the Internet is an excellent source of information about weather and weather patterns.

SEPTEMBER 19

In 1965 divers found the wreck of Le Chameau, which went down during a storm in August 1725 at Kelpy Cove, Cape Breton Island. Its cargo, which was the payroll for French troops in New France, included 11 000 silver coins and 3000 gold coins valued at $250 000.

Treasure Hunt

Materials Needed

Bristol board

dice

markers

Directions:

On a piece of Bristol board, draw a path of squares and label the first square "Start" and the final square "Treasure Recovered." Have the children create a series of task cards with such directions as:

You find two gold coins near the wreck – move forward two spaces.

Place the pile of task cards on the game board and have each player roll the dice. He/she then moves his marker the appropriate number of spaces and picks up and follows the directions on a task card. The first player to reach the square marked "Treasure Recovered" wins.

OCTOBER

OCTOBER 4

Although the Saxby Gale did not occur until October 4th, 1869, the story begins a year earlier, in November 1868, when Lieutenant Saxby of the Royal Navy predicted that at 7 am on October 5, 1869, there would be an intense storm and unusually high tides.

Only one day early, in the afternoon of October 4, 1869, the skies over the Bay of Fundy darkened and by evening the wind was blowing with hurricane force. The coast of New Brunswick was severely battered as tides rose above all previous records.

Weird Weather Wonders

Set up a place in your classroom where the children can collect and display pictures and stories of "Weird Weather Wonders."

OCTOBER 9

On this day in 1002, Leif Erikson and his band of Vikings established a settlement at what is now L'Anse aux Meadows in Newfoundland. An authenticated site of a Norse settlement in North America, this World Heritage Site has been excavated and reconstructed by archaeologists. Visitors can see completed replicas of sod buildings and numerous artifacts.

For more information, contact:

Department of Development
Tourism Branch
P.O. Box 8700
St. John's, Nfld. A1B 4J6
http://whc.unesco.org/en/list/4
whc.unesco.org/en/list/4

OCTOBER 14

In 1926 A. A. Milne's *Winnie the Pooh* was published.

A Scene From Pooh

Read *Winnie the Pooh*, then invite the children to dress as their favourite characters and share their favourite scenes from the story.

OCTOBER 15

Poetry Day

"Even when poetry has meaning, as it usually has, it may be unadvisable to draw it out…Perfect understanding will sometimes almost extinguish pleasure." – A. E. Housman

OCTOBER 19

In 1752, Benjamin Franklin flew a homemade kite during a thunderstorm. The kite was struck by a bolt of lightning, which then travelled down the kite to a key at its end. There was a spark! The spark proved that lightning is electricity. (It also proved that one should not fly a kite during a thunderstorm!)

Lightning Facts

* Every year Toronto's CN Tower is struck by lightning about 65 times.
* There are 100 lightning flashes every second of every day.
* Lightning bolts can be several kilometres in length or just as thick as your finger.
* A single bolt of lightning contains enough electricity to provide power to an average home for two weeks.

"The reason lightning doesn't strike twice in the same place is that the same place isn't there the second time." – Willie Tyler

But former Shenandoah Park Ranger Roy C. Sullivan was struck by lightning seven times.

In 1942 he lost his big toenail.

In 1969 he lost his eyebrows.

In 1970 his left shoulder was seared.

In 1972 his hair was set on fire.

In 1973 a bolt hit him on the head, set his hair on fire, knocked him out of his car, went through both legs and knocked his left shoe off.

In 1976 his ankle was injured.

And in 1977, while fishing, he was struck again and suffered chest and stomach burns.

Sullivan's lightning-burnt ranger hats are in the Guinness World Records Exhibit Halls.

OCTOBER 21

Edison Lamp Day

"The longer it burned, the more fascinated we were…there was no sleep for any of us for 40 hours." – Thomas A. Edison

Thomas Edison did not actually invent the light bulb. In 1829 Humphrey Davey produced an arc light; some years later, Joseph Swan made a crude light bulb, and it was a Canadian student named Henry Woodward who actually patented the electric light bulb. Needing some extra cash, however, Woodward sold his patent to Edison in 1874. Edison's contribution to the light bulb was to improve it by developing a superior filament.

Bright Ideas

Invite students to write letters to Henry Woodward, offering their suggestions for ways he might have raised the money he needed without selling his patent to Thomas Edison.

Books

The Way Things Work, by David Macaulay. Houghton Mifflin, 1988.

OCTOBER 27

Good Bear Day

The teddy bear was named after former United States President Theodore Roosevelt, who was born on October 27th, 1858.

While on a hunting trip, Roosevelt refused to shoot a bear cub that had wandered into the campsite. Hearing this story, a Brooklyn toymaker designed a stuffed bear and hung the sign "Teddy's Bear" around its neck. He displayed it in his shop window and was soon receiving requests to purchase the toy!

Time for Teddy

Invite the children to bring their teddy bears to school. Play a recording of the "Teddy Bears' Picnic", while students listen carefully to the lyrics. Then play the recording again this time having the children creep quietly as they mime the actions of finding the teddy bears at their picnic.

Books

A Bear Called Paddington, by Michael Bond. Dell, 1968.

NOVEMBER
Fall

NOVEMBER 3

Sandwich Day

Sandwich Day is named after John Montague, fourth Earl of Sandwich, who was born on this day in 1718. He is reputed to have asked that slices of bread be brought to the gaming table, rather than interrupt his card games that often lasted as long as 24 hours.

Special Sandwiches

Nowadays, with all the wonderful kinds of bread available – from pita to tortillas – sandwiches can be interesting and even exciting! Work with the class to create the recipe for an extraordinary sandwich.

Sandwiches can tell a story of culture and geography too. Invite the students to bring sandwiches to school and have them prepare a history of the sandwich by considering the composition of the bread and its filling. For example: Did the recipe for this bread originate from a particular culture or country?

NOVEMBER 5

Newfoundland celebrates Bonfire Night

In 1605 Protestantism was the official religion in England. People of other faiths, particularly Catholics, were persecuted and life for them was very difficult. A group of Catholic noblemen decided to blow up the British King and Parliament and concocted what was known as the Gunpowder Plot. But the plot was uncovered and Guy Fawkes, one of the conspirators, was discovered in the basement of the Parliament Building before he could ignite the 36 barrels of gunpowder that had been hidden there. Fawkes and the other plotters were executed for treason.

Since then November 5th has been known as Guy Fawkes Day and his ragged effigy is burned each year on bonfires throughout England. Fireworks are also set off to celebrate the "burning of the guy."

Immigrants to Newfoundland brought the bonfire custom with them. The significance of Guy Fawkes has been replaced by the bonfire itself, usually a collection of wood, rubbish and dead leaves. But sometimes a scarecrow-like figure called "the guy" is included as well.

NOVEMBER 9

In 1976 Smokey the Bear died in the Washington Zoo. As a cub, Smokey had been rescued from a raging forest fire and became a symbol of the American effort to fight forest fires.

Fire Facts

Fire prevention – at home, at school and in forests – continues to be a major concern. By now the children will probably have experienced a fire drill at school and will know enough about fire prevention to appreciate a visit from a representative of your local Fire Fighters Association or the Department of Lands and Forests.

Extended Activity

Following the visit, have the students design fire prevention posters. Set up a display of the posters in your classroom or in the school foyer.

NOVEMBER 14

In 1606, at Port Royal (now Halifax), Nova Scotia, Marc Lescarbot's *Theatre of Neptune* staged the first dramatic production in the New World.

The Neptune Theatre's productions are still known across Canada.

"I write fiction because it's a way of making statements I can disown, and I write plays because dialogue is the most respectable way of contradicting myself" – Tom Stoppard

NOVEMBER 17

In 1988 a group of children in San Antonio, Texas, put together and sold a cookbook just for kids called *An Apple a Day*. Money from the sale was donated to a children's hospital.

Kids Can Cook

Ask each child to print his/her favourite recipe for your own classroom cookbook. Include their personal comments, describing why they like each recipe. Decide how to sell the books and where to donate the proceeds.

NOVEMBER 22

On this day in 1917, the National Hockey League was organized by delegates from Montreal, Quebec, Ottawa and Toronto. The league launched its first season on December 19, 1917, in which four teams (two from Montreal, one from Ottawa and one from Toronto) played a 22-game schedule.

Hockey Heroes

Hockey Hotshots, edited by Bennett Wayne. *Target Series.* Easton, Garrard, 1977.

Gretzky! Gretzky! Gretzky!, by Meguido Zola. *Picture Life Series.* Watts, 1983.

NOVEMBER 24

In 1826 Carlo Collodi, the author of *Pinocchio*, was born.

Pinocchio Puppet Show

Read *Pinocchio*, then divide the class into groups and have each produce a puppet show based on the story.

NOVEMBER 25

St. Catherine's Day

St. Catherine, a fourth century Christian martyr, is the patron saint of virgins and philosophers.

It is said that Marguerite Bourgeoys, a teacher who came to Quebec in the seventeenth century, let her students pull toffee in honor of St. Catherine. St. Catherine's day, therefore, traditionally involves pulling toffee and has become known as La Tire Sainte-Catherine.

At one time, it was also traditional to organize balls and other match-making activities on St. Catherine's Day for single women who wanted to find husbands.

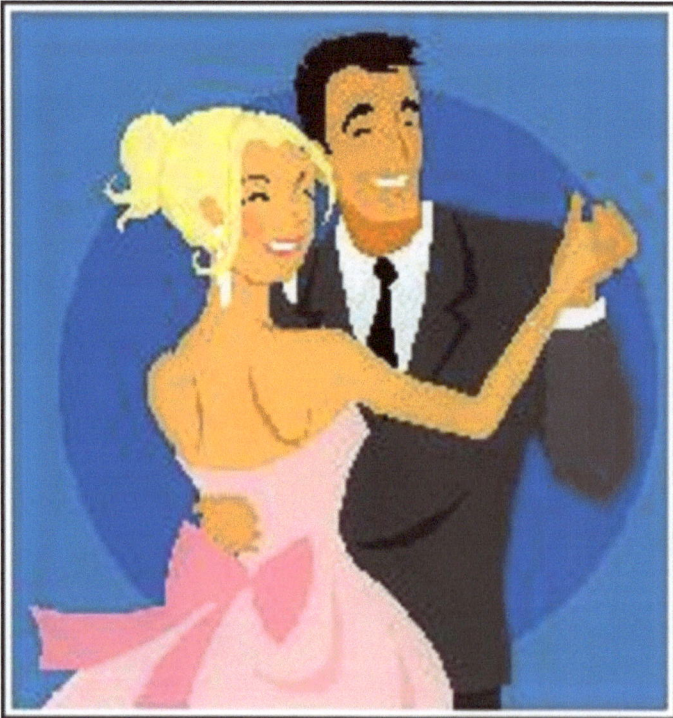

NOVEMBER 30

In 1954 Ann Hodges was sitting in her home in Sylacauga, Alabama, when she was suddenly jolted to her feet. Her left hand and hip hurt and there was a large hole in the ceiling. On the floor lay a large rock – still warm to the touch. It was a meteorite!

WEIRD WEATHER WONDERS

* On November 12, 1883, showers of meteors were seen all over North America. They were described as "a giant umbrella with flaming spokes."
* Between 200 and 2000 meteorites fall to earth each day.
* 90 000 t of micrometeorites (dust particles) fall to earth each day.
* A meteorite strikes a human being roughly once every 10 000 years.
* Meteorites form craters when they strike the ground. Most craters become filled in and disappear. However, there is a meteorite crater in Winslow, Arizona, that measures 1345 m wide and was formed 25 000 years ago

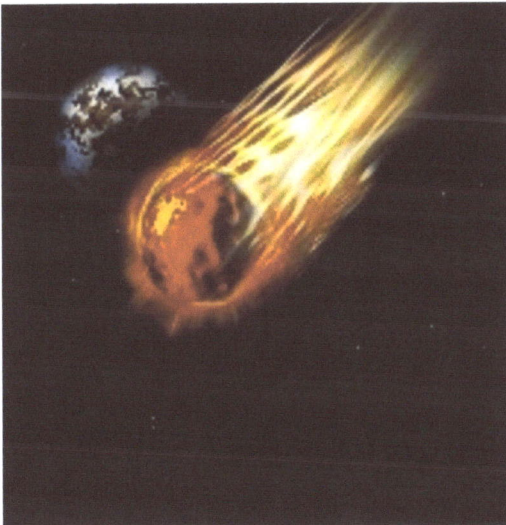

DECEMBER

DECEMBER 1

Every year on this day, the Parkway Mall in Saint John, New Brunswick, erects a large Christmas tree called the Tree of Love. Every time someone gives blood during the month of December, he/she is honoured by having an ornament hung on the tree.

DECEMBER 6

In 1917 the Halifax Explosion took place. This was the single greatest man-made explosion in history prior to Hiroshima.

The explosion took place during World War I, when the French freighter Mont Blanc, loaded with munitions for France, collided with the Norwegian collier Imo in Halifax Harbour. There is no one explanation as to why the collision occurred. It appears to have been caused by a tragic series of coincidences, human error and inexplicable decisions by the two captains involved.

* Between 2000 and 3000 people were killed; some vanished, never to be seen again; more than 10 000 were injured; approximately 200 were blinded.
* More than 12 000 buildings within a 25 km radius were seriously damaged; 1600 were destroyed.

Books

Barometer Rising, by Hugh MacLennan. Gage, 1969.

DECEMBER 10

United Nations Human Rights Day. On this day in 1948, the United Nations Declaration of Human Rights was adapted.

All human beings are born free and equal in dignity and rights…Everyone has the right to freedom of thought…Everyone has the right to freedom of opinion and expression. – United Nations Declaration of Human Rights, 1948.

Books

I Have a Dream, by Margaret Davidson. Scholastic, 1986.

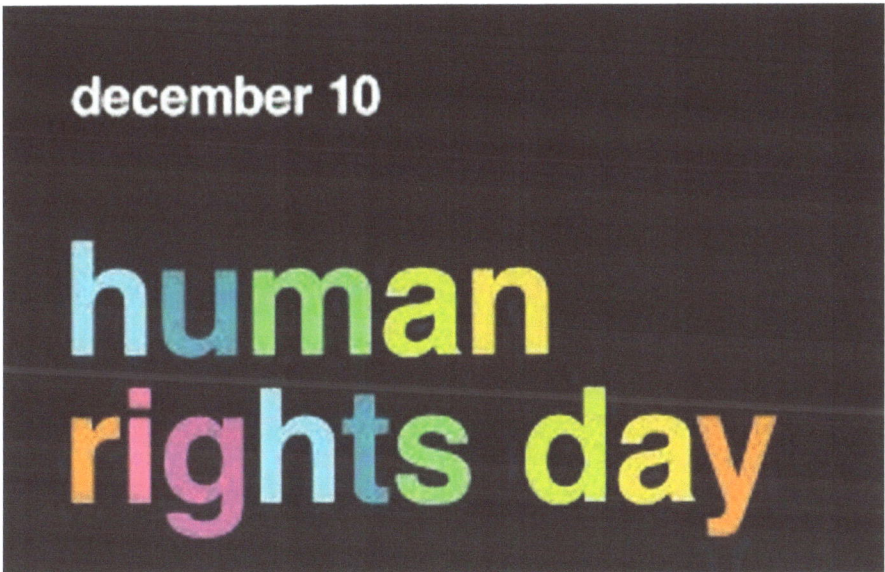

DECEMBER 15

In 1964, the House of Commons voted to adopt the red-and-white maple leaf design as a replacement for the Red Ensign and Union Jack on Canada's flag. It became Canada's flag officially in 1965.

Family Flags

Invite students to design a flag for the class or a flag for their families. Have them present and explain their flags, then mount them on a bulletin board in the classroom.

DECEMBER 21

Winter Solstice

Winter arrives today! To welcome winter, decorate the classroom with snowflakes.

Snowflakes

Materials needed:
  small dried white pasta (in a variety of shapes)
  waxed paper
  white glue
  thread

Directions:

Have students cover their work surface with waxed paper and distribute several pieces of pasta and some glue to each student. Have them glue the shapes together to make snowflakes, making sure that all gaps between the pieces are filled with glue.

Carefully collect the snowflakes and glue a length of thread to each. Hang the snowflakes from the ceiling and lighting fixtures.

Extended Activity

Play recordings of seasonal music and read selections from *The Secret Language of Snow*, by Terry T. Williams and Ted Major.

DECEMBER 24

In 1818 on this night in Austria, Franz Gruber composed the music for the carol "Silent Night".

DECEMBER 25

Christians celebrate Christmas.

DECEMBER 26

Black North Americans begin their celebrations of Kwanza, an African harvest festival of feasting and gift giving.

DECEMBER 27

In 1822 French scientist Louis Pasteur was born.

Milk is now safe to drink because of Pasteur's process of pasteurization, which destroys harmful bacteria.

In fact, Pasteur was so involved in his work that he carried a portable microscope with him whenever he was invited to dine at friends' homes, to see if the food they served was safe to eat,

Books

A Short History of Medicine, by Erwin Ackerknecht. John Hopkins, 1982.

DECEMBER 31

New Year's Eve

In 1857 Ottawa was chosen as the capital of Canada by Queen Victoria.

JANUARY 1

On this day in 1941, the *CBC* introduced its own national news service, with Lorne Greene as announcer.

JANUARY 5

In 1927 the marshmallow was invented.

Distribute marshmallows to the children and ask them to describe what they look, smell, feel and taste like. Then ask: If they were to invent a new snack food, what would it be? How would it look, feel, smell, taste? What name would they give their new creation?

Extended Activity

How would they persuade people to try their new snack food? They may want to design a poster, sing a jingle or create a video.

JANUARY 6

In 1918, during the First World War, a Canadian pilot named Makepeace and an American captain named Hedley were flying a plane 454 metres over German territory.

In an effort to shake off German attack planes, Makepeace took his plane into a nearly vertical dive. The sudden movement so shocked Hedley that he was pulled out of his seat and out of the plane. Makepeace rapidly descended several hundred metres and then levelled off, creating a suction so strong that Hedley was pulled back and landed on the tail of the airplane. He eventually managed to climb back into his seat and the two landed safely behind Allied lines.

JANUARY 11

In 1815 Canada's first prime minister, Sir John A. Macdonald, was born in Glasgow, Scotland.

Sir William Samuel Stephenson was also born on this day in Winnipeg in 1896. Although he is best known as the master spy Intrepid, he also invented a wireless photography transmitter that enabled newspapers to reproduce pictures instantly.

Today, too, is an important anniversary for Canadian Gareth Wood, who in 1986 was one of three explorers who reached the South Pole on foot. The group was retracing the route followed by Captain Robert Scott.

Invite students to select and learn more about one of these Canadians. Have them do library or internet research to prepare an oral report.

JANUARY 12

In 1628 Charles Perrault, collector of the *Mother Goose* tales, was born.

Invite the children to select a scene from their favourite *Mother Goose* story. Have them illustrate the scene on a piece of construction paper cut to the size and shape of a coat hanger. Attach their drawings to hangers and suspend the hangers in the classroom for an exciting display.

Books

Sing a Song of Mother Goose, by Barbara Reid. Scholastic, 1987.

JANUARY 18

In 1917 the Income Tax Act was proclaimed in Canada as a temporary measure to finance World War I.

JANUARY 19

In 1989, Heather Erxleben became Canada's first woman combat soldier.

Although never in such an official capacity, women have long played important roles in military combat. Joan of Arc, Florence Nightingale, Molly Pitcher and Canada's Laura Secord all have a special place in history.

Have students research the accomplishments of these extraordinary women.

Extended Activity

After they have completed their research, students may be interested in assuming the roles of these women. Have other students act as reporters and assign them the task of interviewing these women from history.

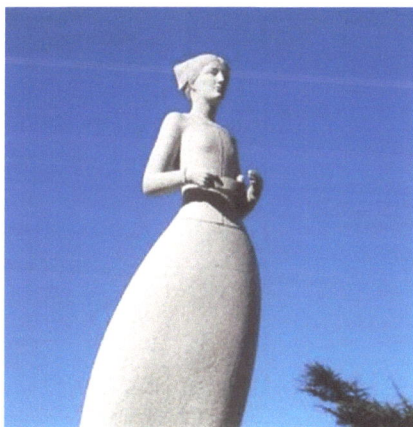

JANUARY 23

In 1878 Louis Riel, then the Métis leader of the first provisional government in the Red River Colony, Rupert's land, was released from a Quebec mental hospital after almost two years' confinement. Riel had been hospitalized after becoming convinced that he was a prophet.

JANUARY 27

In 1931 author Mordecai Richler was born in Montreal.

Read *Jacob Two-Two and the Dinosaur* or *Jacob Two Two Meets the Hooded Fang* with your students.

Ask students to select a character from the story and plan a birthday party for him/her. Whom would they invite? What activities would they organize? What would they serve to eat? Ask them to explain their choices.

JANUARY 30

In 1730 Czar Peter II of Russia died of smallpox on his wedding day.

FEBRUARY

FEBRUARY 1

In 1958 James Gladstone, the former president of the Indian Association of Alberta, was the first native Canadian to become a senator. He spoke in Blackfoot during his first speech in the Senate: "… to place in the official debates a few words in the language of my people."

FEBRUARY 9

In 1883 the first public library in Ontario was opened in Guelph.

Scavenger Hunt

A library is a fascinating place to visit! With help from your school librarian, create a scavenger hunt for the children. Divide the class into teams and provide each with a list of items to find. For older students, the items may be couched as clues.

Distribute bookmarks to everyone!

FEBRUARY 11

In 1922 the discovery of insulin was announced in Toronto. Insulin, which is now used in the treatment of diabetes, was discovered by a research team composed of Frederick Banting, Charles Best, James Collip and James MacLeod. Banting, because the research sprang from his idea, was awarded the Nobel Prize in medicine in 1933.

FEBRUARY 14

In 1925 Valentine Valentine, an American insurance salesman, was born.

For Your Valentine

Have the children arrange bits and pieces of glitter, feathers, fabric and lace on sheets of wax paper. Place a second sheet of wax paper on top of each and press the two together with a warm iron. Then have the children each cut two large heart shapes out of folded construction paper and cut a window in each to frame the wax paper art. Sandwich the art between the hearts and glue everything together.

Children may want to compose a special message to go with their valentines.

FEBRUARY 16

In 1984 Canadian speed-skater Gaetan Boucher won his second gold medal at the Winter Olympics in Sarajevo, Yugoslavia.

Take your class ice-skating today! They'll have fun and get some good exercise at the same time.

FEBRUARY 20

A Mexican farmer named Dionisio Pulido would definitely want this item included in your "Weird Weather Wonders" collection! He witnessed the birth of a volcano!

In 1943, while working in his field, Pulido noticed a crack almost 50 cm long, in the ground. The land surrounding the crack appeared to be bulging and rising. Nobody slept that night. As the frightened villagers waited and watched, the crack spewed out ashes, cinders and fumes. Within ten days, the Paricutin Volcano was 1572 m high and its explosive sounds could be heard in Mexico City, nearly 300 km away.

Volumes About Volcanoes

* When volcanoes erupt, red-hot lava (liquid rock) flows from the top. The lava is contained in chambers deep below the surface and is forced up a pipe-like passage.
* There are about 500 volcanoes in the world.
* Volcanic eruptions are caused by the movement of large plates that constitute the earth's surface.
* The most destructive volcanic eruption in recent history occurred when Krakotoa in Indonesia exploded on August 27, 1883. However, in about 1645 BCE, an eruption five times more powerful than Krakotoa occurred in Greece. The remains of the volcano can be seen on the island of Santorini.
* The volcanoes of Hawaii and Sicily's Mount Etna are called quiet volcanoes because they do not explode; gases and steam are able to escape easily.
* The eruption of Mount St. Helens in the USA on May 18, 1980, was predicted by scientists who had been studying it since 1969.

FEBRUARY 23

In 1909 the first flight in the British Empire of an airplane under its own power was made. The plane, the Silver Dart, was piloted by John A. D. McCurdy of Baddeck, Nova Scotia, and flew a distance of 800 m at an altitude of about 10 m. McCurdy worked with Alexander Graham Bell (the inventor of the telephone) to develop the Silver Dart.

For more information, teachers may contact:

Alexander Graham Bell National Historic Park
P.O. Box 159
Baddeck, Nova Scotia
B0E 1B0
(902-295-2069)
http://www.tripadvisor.ca/Attraction_Review-g499213-d183419-
Reviews-Alexander_Graham_Bell_National_Historic_Site-
Baddeck_Cape_Breton_Island_Nova_Scoti.html

FEBRUARY 25

In 1841 impressionist painter Pierre Auguste Renoir was born.

The impressionists, as the name suggests, painted their impressions of brush strokes. These were usually light in color so as to capture the quality of the light in the scene.

Renoir was disabled by arthritis. His hands were so crippled that he couldn't grip a paintbrush. To overcome this, he strapped a paintbrush to his hand.

Discuss the qualities of courage and determination shown by Renoir to overcome his disabling arthritis. Then discuss other people who have overcome handicaps, such as Beethoven, John Milton, Helen Keller, Terry Fox and Jim Abbott. When they've completed their research, students can use their material to create a mural or bulletin board display of "profiles in courage."

Books

Louis Braille, by Margaret Davidson. Scholastic, 1971.
The Story of Helen Keller, by Lorena A. Hickok. Scholastic, 1958.

FEBRUARY 27

In 1988 Elizabeth Manley of Ottawa won the silver medal in women's figure skating at the Winter Olympics in Calgary.

MARCH

MARCH 1

In 1890 peanut butter was invented.

PEANUT BUTTER LOGS

Materials needed:
225 g (1-1/2 cups) peanut butter
90 mL (6 tablespoons) honey
225 g (1-1/2 cups) raisins
165 mL (3/4 cups) instant dry milk

Directions:

Blend the peanut butter and the honey together, then work in the powdered milk until the dough is stiff. Knead in the raisins and roll the dough into logs. Chill and slice.

You should have about 30 pieces.

MARCH 2

In 1965 convicted drug smuggler Lucien Rivard escaped from a Montreal jail. It was a crisp, cold day and Rivard had obtained a garden hose, saying he wanted to flood the penitentiary skating rink. It appears, however, that he used the hose to help him climb over the penitentiary wall.

Great Escapes

Ask your school librarian to help you create a display of "great escape" stories.

MARCH 8

International Women's Day is celebrated on the anniversary of the first protest march against terrible working conditions for women textile and garment workers in New York City in 1857. On this day, celebrate the accomplishments of women of all ages.

Books

Dreams Into Deeds, by Linda Peavy. Macmillan, 1985.

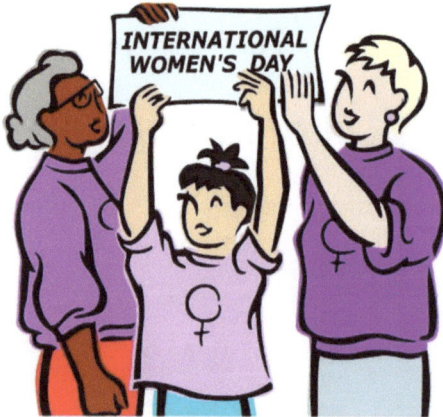

MARCH 10

In 1876 Alexander Graham Bell transmitted the first telephone message. He was preparing to test his new invention (the telephone) when, before he could properly begin, he spilled battery acid on his leg and shouted: "Mr. Watson, come here. I want you."

Tin Can Telephones

Materials needed:
two empty cans
string

Directions:
Punch a hole in the bottom of each can and feed string through each hole to connect the cans. When the string is pulled taut, one student will be able to speak to another by using the cans as a kind of telephone.

Contact the Bell Homestead in Brantford, Ontario, to receive a copy of their newsletter called Bell's Bulletin.
94 Tutela Heights Road
Brantford, Ontario N3T 1A1
(519 – 756-6220)
http://www.brantford.ca/discover/Pages/BellHomestead.as
px

MARCH 11

In 1810 Emperor Napoleon was married by proxy to eighteen-year-old Princess Marie Louise of Austria. (Marie Louise could fold her ears).

MARCH 15

This is Buzzard Day in the town of Hinkley, Ohio. The buzzards (turkey vultures) spend the winter farther south in the Great Smokey Mountains and return home to Hinkley on March 15.

MARCH 17

St. Patrick's Day

Patrick was actually born in Britain. When he was sixteen, he was kidnapped by Irish pirates and sent to Ireland as a slave. He was a shepherd for six years before escaping on a ship bound for Gaul (now France), where he became a priest and later a bishop.

In 432 C.E. the Pope sent Patrick back to Ireland to teach the gospel to the same tribesmen who had kidnapped and enslaved him! Patrick spent nearly thirty years bringing Christianity to the Irish and has remained the beloved patron saint of Ireland.

MARCH 20

This is St. Joseph's Day. Every year on this day since 1776, the swallows have returned to the mission at St. Juan Capistrano, California. The birds travel an estimated 10 000 km from their winter home in Argentina. Fewer and fewer birds are returning, however, and increasing crowds and urban sprawl are blamed.

Spring Watch

Discuss the various occurrences that tell us that spring is on the way, then create a "Spring Watch" bulletin board. When the children notice signs that warmer weather is on the way, have them make drawings or three-dimensional representations of that sign and mount their work on the bulletin board.

MARCH 26

In 1921 the Bluenose was launched at Lunenberg, Nova Scotia.

The Bluenose was the fastest ship in the North Atlantic fishing fleet and won the International Fisherman's Trophy five times. A replica of the Bluenose now resides in Halifax Harbour and its picture appears on the dime.

MARCH 28

In 1658 Jan Amos Komensky's *Visible World of Pictures* was the first book published just for children. Working on the theory that it's easier for young children to remember words when they are accompanied by pictures, he created a pocket-sized book filled with woodcut illustrations. March 28, 1592, is the day Komensky was born. On the anniversary of his birth, Czech children bring flowers and gifts to their teachers.

Picture Books

Share *The Mysteries of Harris Burdick* by Chris Van Allsburg with the class. (This book has beautiful black-and-white woodcut-like drawings.) Encourage the class to write and illustrate their own picture books.

MARCH 29

Your "Weird Weather Wonders" collection would not be complete without an entry on March 29, 1848 – the day Niagara Falls ran dry!

Accustomed to the roar of 155 million litres of water pouring over the Horseshoe Falls every minute, local residents were puzzled by the silence when they awoke to find that the river bed was dry except for a few puddles. At first people enjoyed the novelty of walking on the river bottom without getting their feet wet, but as the day wore on, they became apprehensive about what the sudden disappearance of the water might portend. Later that night, things returned to normal. It was discovered that a huge ice jam had formed near Buffalo and blocked the river completely.

It is unlikely that this will happen again. Niagara Falls is the main source of electricity for both southern Ontario and New York State, so a boom at the entrance of the river has been created to impede the formation of such blockages.

Niagara Note:

As the action and pressure of the water erodes the rock ledge over which it plunges, Niagara Falls is moving upriver at the rate of 91.5 cm every year.

MARCH 31

In 1949 Newfoundland entered the Dominion of Canada as the tenth province.

Invite students to create a birthday card for Canada's youngest province.

Newfoundland/Labrador • Canada

APRIL

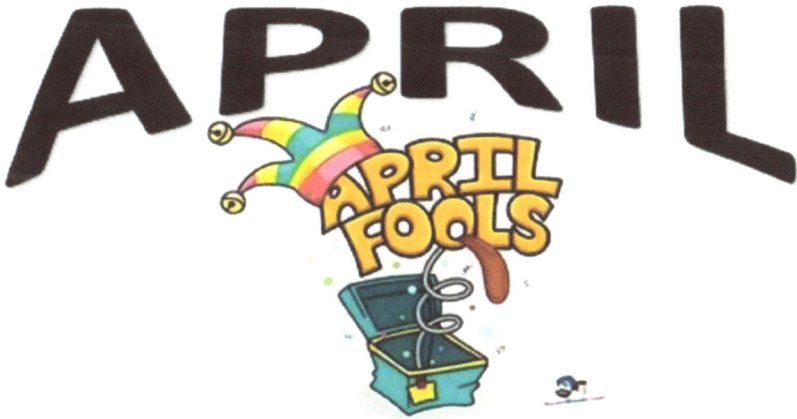

APRIL 1

All Fools' Day

Nobody really knows how All Fools' Day, or April Fools' Day, got started. Some say that on this day Noah sent the first dove from the ark and it returned, unable to find land. Others say that All Fools' Day is an old Celtic heathen festival. A third theory is that it started in France when a new calendar was introduced in 1564. There are records of All Fools' Day celebrations being held throughout Europe during the eighteenth century.

April Fool!

In 1957 as an All Fools' Day joke, British television aired a film showing peasants harvesting spaghetti from trees in the Ticino district of Switzerland. The narrator explained, quite seriously, that the early spring had produced a bumper crop of spaghetti. Afterwards, the BBC was flooded with calls from people wanting to know where they could buy the spaghetti plants. They were told that the plants were not available in England, but that some Americans were experimenting with planting small cans of spaghetti in tomato sauce!

APRIL 2

International Children's Book Day

Hans Christian Andersen was born on this day in 1805, and each year a special poster with bookmarks is produced in his honor for International Children's Book Day. In 1990 it was Canada's turn to design the poster.

POSTER TALES

To mark this special day, invite children to design posters for their favorite Hans Christian Andersen tales. Create a display of the posters in your classroom.

Books

The Steadfast Tin Soldier, by Hans Christian Andersen. Knopf, 1986.
The Ugly Duckling, by Hans Christian Andersen. Knopf, 1986.

APRIL 11

Holocaust Remembrance Day

The word holocaust – which means wholesale sacrifice or destruction – has come to describe the fate of more than six million Jewish people who were put to death by the Nazis in Germany and in many of the countries overrun by the Nazis, during the Second World War (1939-45).

Holocaust Remembrance Day is a day of reflection.
In remembrance lies the hope that never again will such a tragedy be allowed to happen.

Imagine you are allowed only one bag for all of your possessions. A soldier holding a rifle orders you to quickly board a cattle car. The door locks and the train pulls out slowly. You have no idea where you are going or when the train will stop.

APRIL 12

In 1967 the House of Commons unanimously voted to make "O Canada" our country's national anthem. "O Canada" was composed by Calixa Lavalee and first played in 1880 at a banquet in Quebec City.

Take a few moments today to sing "O Canada" with your class!

APRIL 14

Baseball season is here.

Theoretically, it should be warm enough for baseball, which domed stadia notwithstanding, is primarily an outdoor sport! But this isn't always the case. In 1953 a snowfall forced postponement of the Boston Red Sox opener at Fenway Park. Pitcher Mel Parnell donned skis and amused everyone by pitching snowballs before the game was called off.

Books

Bruce Weber's Inside Baseball, by Bruce Weber, Scholastic, 1990.

APRIL 15

In 1452 Leonardo da Vinci was born.

"I have offended God and mankind because my work didn't reach the quality it should have." – Leonardo da Vinci

Da Vinci considered all arts and sciences to be branches of a single tree of learning and had interests in anatomy, engineering, printing and architecture. His inventions often weren't realized but he did conceptualize the helicopter and an underwater breathing device. He also invented the parachute, but is best remembered for his paintings, including *The Last Supper* and *Mona Lisa*. Da Vinci's notebooks remain as a permanent record of his inventiveness. They are handwritten – backwards!

SECRET CODES

The children can create their own secret messages by printing on paper held perpendicular to a mirror.

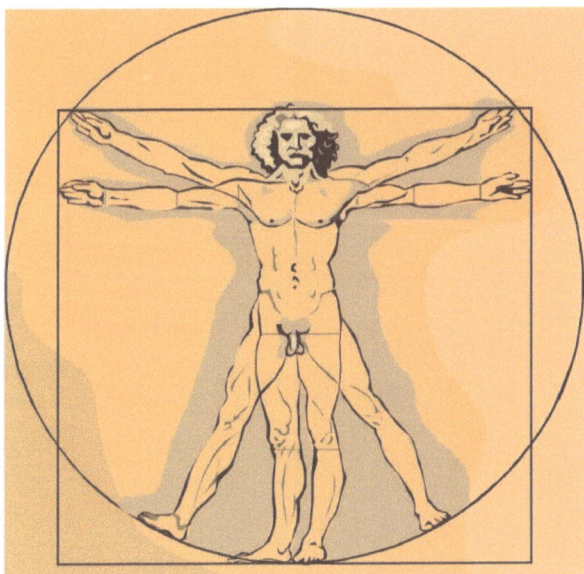

APRIL 18

In 1793 the first newspaper in what is now Ontario was published.

The Upper Canada Gazette was a four-page weekly that included government announcements, news about the French Revolution and stories reprinted from European periodicals. The paper was initially printed by Louis Roy, the first government printer of Upper Canada, and ceased publication in 1845.

What's News?

Divide the class into small groups and provide each with a newspaper. Ask them to find the following items:
* the name of your town
* today's date
* a number that is equal to the age of the youngest person in the group
* the funniest comic strip
* a picture of an animal
* something good to eat
* a telephone number
* news about the weather
* something they would like to buy

APRIL 19

In 1729 Duke Antonio Fernando, who never drank liquor because a fortune-teller had warned that alcohol would kill him, caught fire and burned to death after rubbing his sore muscles with alcohol.

APRIL 22

Earth Day was first observed in 1970 to celebrate the equinoxes and stand for balance and harmony on earth.

Did You Know...

* that recycling one tonne of paper saves about 17 trees?
* that recycling one aluminum can or one glass bottle saves enough energy to power a television set for three hours?
* that twenty recycled cans can be made with the same energy needed to make one can from raw materials?
* that 60 per cent of what people throw away can be recycled?
* that wax paper is biodegradable?

Books

The Giving Tree, by Shel Silverstein. HarperCollins, 1964.

APRIL 29

In 1939 an Indian elder reported seeing an ogopogo in the North Saskatchewan River near Rocky Mountain House, Alberta.

Chief Walking Eagle was crossing the river at a place called the old ford when he saw the monster. He said that the creature chased him across the ford and described it as being "as big as an elephant, having horns instead of ears, and eyes as big as plates, but no tusks or trunk."

Monster Madness

Introduce your students to some of Canada's mythical creatures, such as the sasquatch and ogopogo. Then have the class use recycled plastic containers, pop cans, etc. to create their own mythical monsters.

Older students may want to prepare a tabloid describing "the creatures that lurk in Canadian forests."

MAY 1

May Day

In 1990, after hearing reports of men wearing white robes and brandishing smoking crosses, police in Worcestershire, England, raced to a field thinking that the Ku Klux Klan were having a gathering. Instead of the Klan, however, they found a group of local beekeepers, all wearing white overalls and using smoke in an effort to calm the bees!

MAY 2

In 1936 Sergei Prokofiev's symphony *Peter and the Wolf*, premiered in Moscow.

The music to *Peter and the Wolf* is very expressive. Each instrument represents a different character. Have students close their eyes and listen to a selection from *Peter and the Wolf*. What can they imagine happening as the music plays? Are the instruments appropriate for the characters?

Algonquin Park in Ontario offers visitors an opportunity to attend a wolf howl. For more information, see:
http://www.algonquinpark.on.ca/visit/programs/wolf-howls.php

Wolf Wisdom

* Wolf-pack members take turns babysitting each other's pups while the rest of the pack finds food.
* Wolves teach their pups how to hunt; they play hunting and tracking games with them.
* Before a hunt, wolves may hold a "pep rally" with each wolf howling in a different key. This is to warn other wolves to stay out of their territory.

MAY 4

In 1776 invisible ink was used for the first time in official documents. During the American Revolution, a member of the American Committee of Secret Correspondence was sent to France to buy arms. Fearing capture and interrogation by the British, he had his instructions written in invisible ink.

Invisible Ink

Children can write their own invisible messages with a paintbrush and citrus juice on absorbent paper. To read the messages, hold the paper over a light bulb.

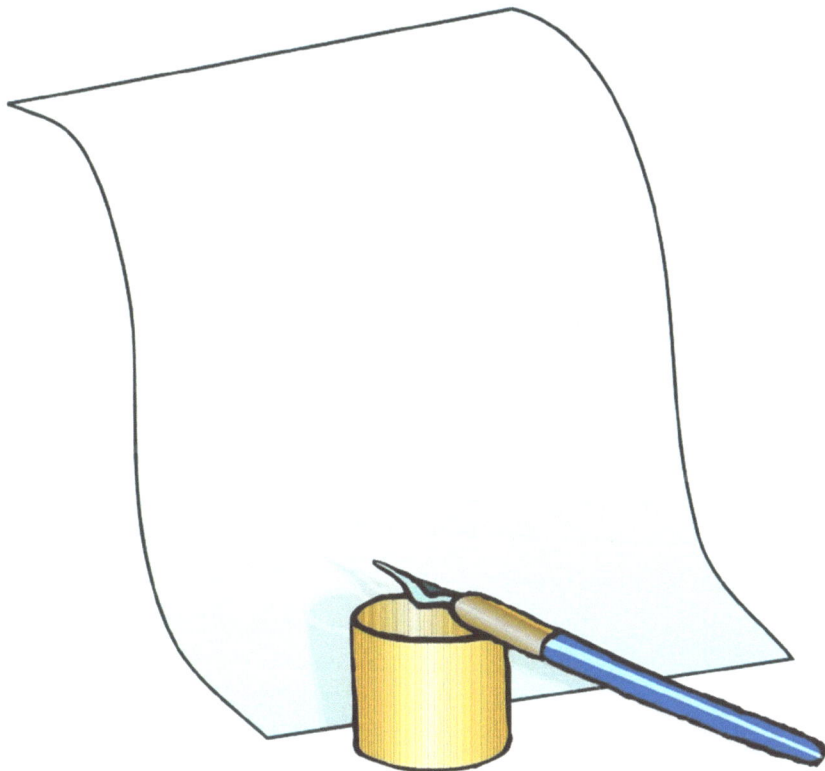

MAY 7

In 1920 the Group of Seven, Canada's famous landscape painters – Franklin Carmichael, Lawren Harris, A.Y. Jackson, Franz Johnston, Arthur Lismer, J E.H. MacDonald and F.H. Varley – held their first exhibition at what is now the Art Gallery of Ontario. Many of the works of the Group of Seven are on permanent display at the McMichael Gallery in Kleinburg, Ontario.

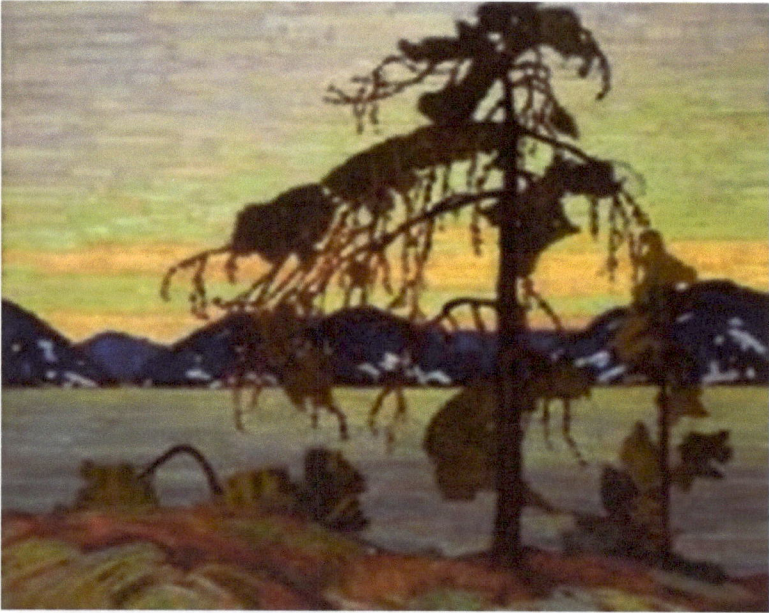

MAY 12

In 1921 author Farley Mowat was born in Belleville, Ontario. He died on May 6, 2014, in Port Hope, Ontario, just 6 days away from his 93rd birthday.

Books

The Dog Who Wouldn't Be, by Farley Mowat. Bantam, 1981.
Owls in the Family, by Farley Mowat. Bantam, 1981.

MAY 14

In 1796 Dr. Edward Jenner, a British physician, administered the first smallpox vaccine.

Jenner noticed that milkmaids almost never got smallpox, a very dangerous disease, but they frequently got cowpox, which was similar, but not life threatening. As an experiment, Jenner injected a boy with fluid from a milkmaid who had cowpox. Then Jenner injected him with the smallpox virus. The boy did not get smallpox!

Nowadays, we take smallpox vaccination and other preventative inoculations for granted. However, in Jenner's day, people were afraid of the first smallpox vaccine. Since the early smallpox serum was derived from cows, they were afraid that their children might start to behave like cows.

MAY 19

On November 18, 1865, Mark Twain's story "The Celebrated Jumping Frog of Calaveras County," was published in the *Saturday Press*.

Every May in honour of Mark Twain, residents of California host the Calaveras County Jumping Frog Jubilee, billed as the "world's premier frog-jumping event."

Canadians too, give frogs a chance to strut their stuff. Every year on the August long weekend, St. Pierre-Jolys, Manitoba, hosts the Frog Follies (Folies Grenouilles). The winner is the frog that covers the greatest distance in three hops. A Canadian record of 449 cm was set in 1985 by a local frog named Tequila.

MAY 20

In 1873, Levi Strauss patented denim pants.

When gold was discovered in California in 1848, thousands of people flooded California looking to make their fortunes. Levi Strauss, a merchant who knew that the miners would need supplies, came with heavy canvas for the miners' tents and covered wagons. It transpired that what the miners really needed was rugged pants, so the enterprising Strauss switched from tents and wagon coverings to pants. The canvas he had brought with him was too stiff to be worn comfortably, so he sent for a different fabric from Nimes, France. He called the material "de Nimes," which means "from Nimes" in French; hence, "denim."

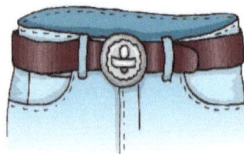

MAY 28

In 1934 the Dionne quintuplets were born near North Bay, Ontario. The five girls, daughters of Oliva and Elzire Dionne, were a $500 million tourist attraction in the province of Ontario during the Depression. They were so tiny at birth that their mother could slip her ring over their hands.

MAY 29

In 1912 Edward W. Bok, editor of *The Ladies' Home Journal,* fired fifteen women on his staff after he caught them dancing "The Turkey Trot" during their lunch break!

MAY 30

In 1672 Czar Peter the Great was born in Russia.

He was unable to grow a beard, so he outlawed beards in his kingdom.

JUNE

JUNE 1

In 1644 the Bishop of Geneva led a procession of 300 people to perform an exorcism of a glacier that was threatening the town of Chamonix on the border between France and Switzerland.

GLACIER LORE

* Glaciers are very much like rivers of ice. They form when snow piles up in mountain hollows, called cirques, where it is gradually compacted into a white substance, not quite snow, yet not quite ice. As the pressure increases, the ice crystals appear to interlock, while water, seeping down from above, refreezes and binds the crystals together. The compacted snow is eventually pressed into clear blue ice.
* The melting and refreezing of the ice underneath the glacier helps it to move.
* Most glaciers move only a metre or so every day; some move more slowly.
* The glacier ends when it gets so warm that the ice melts, or it reaches the sea.

* In 1933 the body of a ram was found at the end of the Lyell Glacier in California. Scientists decided that the ram, which belonged to a species that had been extinct for fifty years, had fallen into a crevasse near the head of the glacier 250 years earlier. It had taken 250 years for the glacier to move the ram's body to the glacier's end-point.
* Canada's most famous glacier is the Columbia Ice Field in Alberta. Visitors can actually go out onto the glacier in a special vehicle designed for that purpose.

JUNE 3

On this day in 1989, it was opening day at the new Sky Dome (now Rogers Centre) in Toronto. Ontario's Premier David Peterson pointed a laser beam upward to open the stadium's focal point – its retractable roof. Performers were drenched and many of the 50 000 spectators sought cover as they were hit by a deluge of water from a fierce rainstorm outside!

The attraction of places such as the Rogers Centre is that sports like baseball and football are no longer dependent upon weather conditions.

Organize the class into small groups and ask them to create a list of activities that are dependent on weather conditions. On the blackboard, draw up a master list of their responses and invite each group to select an item and to brainstorm ways of making it weatherproof. Let each group present what it has done to the rest of the class.

JUNE 6

In 1937 the Salvation Army declared June 6th Doughnut Day, as a means of raising funds during the Great Depression.

The doughnuts originally brought to North America by Dutch settlers weren't as appetizing as they are now. They were flat, fried cakes with uncooked, soggy centres. The hole in the doughnut was the brainchild of 15-year-old Hanson Crockett Gregory in 1847. He used a fork to poke out the centres of the uncooked doughnuts his mother was making. Removing the centre allowed the dough to cook more evenly.

JUNE 9

In 1987 Gatling's Funeral Home in Chicago opened a drive-through service, so that grieving friends, family members and former lovers might view the deceased – by way of a video screen – and pay their respects without having to park their cars!

JUNE 10

In 1918 author and illustrator Maurice Sendak was born.

SENSATIONAL STATIONERY

Read *Where the Wild Things Are* or *In the Night Kitchen* with students. Then have them draw a picture illustrating some aspect of the story, using a black marker or a pencil and making sure that the lines are dark. Use a photocopier to reduce the pictures and print several pieces of personalized stationery for each child.

JUNE 16

In 1988 a bull named Colonel proved there is no substance to the old adage "like a bull in a china shop."

Curious to find out what a bull really would do in a china shop, Grant Burnett, a china shop owner in New Zealand, borrowed Colonel, a 900 kg Hereford bull, and let him loose in the store for three hours. Result: Colonel didn't break anything!

SINGING SAYINGS

Ask students to list some of the popular clichés with which we sprinkle our language, then have them select several of these to compose an original song about language. They may use items in the classroom to provide musical accompaniment.

JUNE 24

Quebec and francophone communities across Canada celebrate the feast day of St. John the Baptist. In the province of Quebec, la Fete de la Saint-Jean-Baptiste is la Fete Nationale, an official holiday.

St. John the Baptist is the patron saint of French Canadians. His birthday is celebrated by parades and bonfires (St. John's fires). In recent years, St. John the Baptist festivities have become a rallying point for nationalist sentiments.

This is also an important day for Newfoundlanders. John Cabot arrived in Newfoundland on June 24, 1497, and planted the British flag on Sugarloaf Mountain. St. John's, Newfoundland, is named for the explorer John Cabot, and June 24th is called Discovery Day!

JUNE 26

In 1284, according to legend, the Pied Piper of Hamelin, Germany, agreed to charm all the rats out of town in exchange for the fee of 1000 guilders. When his fee was not paid, he lured the villagers' children to a mountain where they all disappeared. This was his revenge. ("Pied" means covered with patches.)

PIED PIPER PLAYS

Tell children the story of the *Pied Piper of Hamelin*. Ask them what they think might have happened to the children when they arrived at the mountain and encourage them to share their ideas in the form of a dramatic improvisation or a written sequel to the story.

JULY 1

Canada Day

JULY 5

In 1980, at a World Worm Charming Championship in Cheshire, England, Tom Shufflebotham, a local farmer's son, charmed a record 511 worms out of the ground in the allotted time of 30 minutes. Garden forks or other implements are vibrated in the soil to coax up the worms. Water is not allowed.

JULY 7

In 1887 Marc Chagall was born in Russia. His paintings are a celebration of Russian-Jewish life and include floating bodies and animals with human facial expressions.

PICTURE FILES

While planning for the school year to come, now is a good time to organize a picture file for use in your classroom's creative writing centre. Newspapers, outdated calendars and magazines are a good source. Remove the cutlines (captions) from the pictures, but do not discard them. Laminated pictures of animals, people, scenery, facial expressions and art reproductions are all useful. Following are some suggested activities:

* Match pictures with their cutlines.
* Create a cutline for the picture.
* Write a story about what is happening in the picture.
* Brainstorm 10 words to describe the picture.
* Cut the picture into pieces like a puzzle and reassemble it.
* Write a lost-and-found advertisement for the picture or an object in it.
* Describe how you would begin a conversation with someone in the picture.

JULY 10

In 1931 author and 2013 Nobel Laureate in Literature Alice Munro was born.

JULY 13

In 1816 *The Old Farmer's Almanac* called for rain, snow and hail for July 13th. The forecast had been slipped in by a typesetter who had intended it as a joke; he thought that for sure the editor would catch it, but the editor missed it. The first several copies were printed with the gag forecast included. However, when July 13th arrived, it brought rain, snow and hail. People who had received copies printed before the forecast was revised, swore by *The Old Farmer's Almanac* thereafter!

JULY 17

In 1988 a garden snail named Tracker completed a 33 cm course at Norfolk, England, in 2 minutes, 31 seconds. A silver tankard stuffed with lettuce was presented to him.

JULY 19

In 1938 pilot Douglas "Wrong Way" Corrigan took off for Los Angeles – and landed in Dublin. Corrigan blamed his compass, but skies over New York were clear enough for him to have detected his error visually. It is suspected that he had intended to fly to Ireland all along, but was unable to obtain clearance for the trans-Atlantic flight.

AUGUST

AUGUST 6

In 1867 William Thompson, a Union Pacific telegraph operator in the United States, was ambushed by Cheyenne Indians, shot and scalped. He was roused by the sensation of the knife on his head. He grabbed his scalp from the startled Indian and ran. The warrior did not give chase. Thompson donated his scalp to the Omaha Public Library, where it is on display.

AUGUST 9

In 1987 a woman living in Hamilton, Ontario, got what was probably the shock of her life when she found a 1.8 m boa constrictor peering up from the toilet in her apartment.

AUGUST 16

In 1858 the Bank of Canada was chartered. Royal assent was given to an act to abolish imprisonment for debt.

AUGUST 19

In 1951 Eddie Gaedel, a 108 cm midget, pinch-hit for the St. Louis Browns, who were playing the Detroit Tigers. Wearing number 1/8, the batter with the smallest ever major-league strike zone, walked on four pitches. Following the game, the major-league rules were rewritten to prevent the recurrence of such an event.

AUGUST 22

In 1926 the United States Board of Censorship forced the producers of the film *The Scarlet Letter* (based on the novel by Hawthorne) to make some changes. Among other things, they insisted that Hester Prynne get married.

AUGUST 23

In 1691 explorer Henry Kelsey became the first white man to take part in an Indian buffalo hunt in what is now Saskatchewan.

Buffalo and the buffalo hunt are an integral part of the history of western Canada. In 1981 the Head-Smashed-In Buffalo Jump in southern Alberta was designated a World Heritage Site by UNESCO.

For more information contact:

Head-Smashed-In Buffalo Jump,
Interpretive Centre,
c/o Area Manager,
Historic Sites Service
P. O. Box 1977
Fort Macleod, Alberta
T0L 0Z0
(403-553-2731)
http://history.alberta.ca/headsmashedin/default.aspx

AUGUST 30

In 1988 Kenji Kawamura purchased a 22-wheeled Cadillac. "The Hollywood Dream" could accommodate fifty passengers, and was equipped with a swimming pool, a putting green, a satellite receiving dish, six telephones and a helicopter landing pad.

WWW.JAYOHRBERG.COM

Visit Joan at her FaceBook Page
At her Blogsite
http://joanocallaghan.blogspot.ca/
or Tweet with @JoanOcallaghan

About the Author

Joan O'Callaghan is a recipient of the Golden Apple Award from Queen's University Faculty of Education for Excellence in Teaching; named Professor of the Year by OISE/UT Students Council, as well as Most Engaging English Instructor and Most Inspirational Instructor.

She is the author of three educational books as well as two e-shorts: "George" and "For Elise" (Carrick Publishing).

Her short story "Stooping to Conquer" appeared in the 2012 Anthology *EFD1: Starship Goodwords* (Carrick Publishing).

In 2013, her story "Sugar 'N' Spice" appeared in the Crime Anthology *Thirteen*, by the Mesdames of Mayhem (Carrick Publishing). This anthology received two nominations for the coveted Arthur Ellis Award for Best Short Story.

In 2014, Joan's story "Runaway" was a runner-up for the Bony Pete Award for short crime fiction, and was subsequently published in *World Enough And Crime*, Carrick Publishing, 2014.

Her Flash Fiction "Torch Song for Two Voices" won first place in the 2014 Polar Expressions contest, and was lead story in *That Golden Summer*, Polar Expressions.

In addition, "Thrice the Brinded Cat" was published in *13 O'Clock*, Carrick Publishing, 2015, and "A Good Beginning" appeared in *Over My Dead Body*, 2015, an online magazine.

www.ingramcontent.com/pod-product-compliance
Lightning Source LLC
Chambersburg PA
CBHW042128080426
42735CB00001B/9